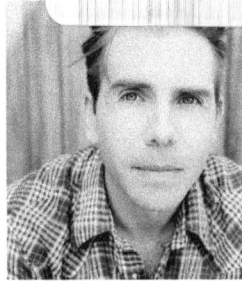

MATTHEW RYAN's work includes: *Kelly* (Queensland Theatre Company 2012), *boy girl wall* co-written with Lucas Stibbard (The Escapists/Melbourne Theatre Company 2012/Critical Stages National Australian Tour 2012/ La Boite Theatre Company 2011/Hothouse Theatre 2011/Adelaide Fringe 2010/Metro Arts 2010/2009), *The Harbinger* co-written with David Morton (Dead Puppet Society/La Boite Theatre Company 2012), *French Twist* (Queensland Theatre Company 2011 as 'Sacre Bleu'), *Attack Of The Attacking Attackers!* (The Escapists/La Boite Theatre Company 2008), *Summer Wonderland* (La Boite Theatre Company 2007), *Chasing The Whale* (La Boite Theatre Company 2005/ATYP 2000 as 'The Dance of Jeremiah') and *So You Die A Little* co-written with Tony Brockman (Pandemonium Theatre 1998). Matthew has developed a series of works for young performers through Backbone Youth Arts called *Plays From The Top Of The Stairs*. Matthew received the Queensland Theatre Company's George Landen Dann award for *Chasing The Whale* (as 'The Dance of Jeremiah') in 2000, the Matilda Award for Best New Australian Work for *Attack Of The Attacking Attackers!* in 2008 and the Matilda Award for Best Independent Production in 2011 for *boy girl wall*. Matthew is a co-founder of the award winning theatre-making group The Escapists.

LUCAS STIBBARD makes theatre and performance, this has included work nationally and internationally as an actor, performer, writer, puppeteer, director, facilitator, host, dramaturge and memorably as stage manager for The Lala Parlour burlesque troupe. As a writer Lucas is best know for boy girl wall that he co-wrote with Matthew Ryan. Other works have included short stories for Stage X, articles for the union journal and a story in Men of Letters. Lucas has worked a performer for QTC, MTC, La Boite, Bell Shakespeare, STCSA and Windmill amongst others and is one of the founders of The Escapists, a collective whose work has included the Helpmann Award nominated boy girl wall, Elephant Gun, The Prometheus Project and the upcoming works Packed and Suburbia.

boy girl wall

MATTHEW RYAN AND LUCAS STIBBARD

Based on a story by Lucas Stibbard

CURRENCY PRESS
The performing arts publisher

CURRENCY PLAYS

First published in 2012
by Currency Press Pty Ltd,
PO Box 2287, Strawberry Hills, NSW, 2012, Australia
enquiries@currency.com.au
www.currency.com.au
in association with
The Escapists

NATIONAL LIBRARY OF AUSTRALIA CIP DATA

Author:	Ryan, Matthew, 1978–
Title:	boy girl wall / Matthew Ryan and Lucas Stibbard.
ISBN:	9780868199559 (pbk.)
Series:	Current theatre series.
Subjects:	Love—Drama.
	Neighbours—Drama.
Other authors / Contributors:	
	Stibbard, Lucas.
Dewey Number:	A822.4

Typeset by Dean Nottle for Currency Press.
Cover design by Katy Wall for Currency Press.
Front cover image design by Sean Dowling.

Currency Press acknowledges the Traditional Owners of the Country on which we live and work. We pay our respects to all Aboriginal and Torres Strait Islander Elders, past and present.

Contents

boy girl wall was first produced by The Escapists for Metro Arts Independents, Brisbane, on 14 August 2009 with the following cast and creative team:

NARRATOR	Lucas Stibbard
MUSICIAN	Neridah Waters

Realisers, Matthew Ryan, Lucas Stibbard, Neridah Waters, Sarah Winter
Composer, Neridah Waters
Lighting Designer, Keith Clark

The Escapists produced a season of *boy girl wall* for the Adelaide Fringe Festival and a return season at Metro Arts in 2010. It was produced for mainstage seasons at La Boite Theatre Company and HotHouse Theatre in 2011. It was produced for Melbourne Theatre Company's Lawler Studio Season and a National Australian Tour (through Critical Stages) in 2012.

The set was redesigned by Jonathon Oxlade in 2011 for mainstage productions and all subsequent seasons.

The Escapists are Keith Clark, Jonathon Oxlade, Matthew Ryan, Lucas Stibbard, Neridah Waters and Sarah Winter.

CHARACTERS

NARRATOR, plays all roles

SETTING

The set of the original production was a simple black space with corners and edges highlighted with chalk. The redesign consisted of a collection of chalkboards rising up as a back wall and one large chalkboard as the stage.

PRE-SHOW PHONE WARNING

NARRATOR: [*pre-recorded*] Evening, everyone. Thanks for coming and welcome. The show is about to start so if everyone could just turn off your mobile phones that'd be aces—unless you need to leave it on for some kind of emergency—like you left the kids with a babysitter and you're only now realising that those scabs on her arm were track marks. Or like... This is a true story actually. When I worked as an usher there was this one night that this girl's phone went off, full volume in the middle of the show. She answered it, started talking excitedly, got her friend out of the audience. They both chatted loudly and then walked out of the theatre. I followed them out and, puffed up with self-importance I demanded to know what was so important as to NOT-TURN-OFF-YOUR-MOBILE-PHONE-HOW-DARE-SHE-RUIN-THE-MAGIC-OF-THEATRE. Her answer—'I just got confirmation, they've found a match and I'm getting my new kidney'. So she and her friend left smiling and I was reminded that as fun as this is, it's not going to change the world. Or help you regulate electrolytes. So, yeah, phones off unless you left your kids with a crack whore or you're waiting for a vital organ. Cheers for listening and enjoy the show.

1. THIS IS NOT A LOVE STORY

The NARRATOR *appears in the audience wearing a suit. He approaches the stage.*

NARRATOR: This is not a love story. At no point will Colin Firth come striding over the hill towards his poor but willful girl in an empire line, who has selflessly put her family first. Leonardo DiCaprio won't meet a plucky Kate Winslet aboard a doomed ship. Nor will said doomed ship meet an iceberg resulting in the selfish bitch not sharing her floaties with him. Women hired to look after the children of brooding Austrian sea captains won't sing songs about singing songs and then outwit Nazis with their friends from a nunnery. This is not a love story. This is a story about love. Which is to say, real

1

love. Which is to say, it's a million moments of misery and one good one.

2. BOY

NARRATOR: Consider light.

> *He throws some light from his hand into a light bulb that hangs in the middle of the space. The bulb lights up.*

> *He takes out some chalk and starts doing maths and diagrams on the back wall/chalkboards.*

Now, it can be found as a by-product of our sun's nuclear reactions and is a form of electromagnetic radiation. That radiation is held to travel at a constant speed of 1,079,252,848.8 kilometres per hour and will travel the distance from sun to the Earth (not to scale) in approximately 8.3 minutes. Which means that the sun you see at any time is actually the sun as it was 8.3 minutes ago. Let's go out further. Say thirty light years. Now that being the distance that sunlight will travel at our understood constant of 1,079,252,848.8 kilometres per hour in 30 years. Or. Lots. And if you happened to be viewing the Earth from that distance and if you had a sufficiently powerful instrument of observation to do so, you would actually be seeing the Earth as it was thirty years ago. So, let us imagine that an alien observer happened to train their fantastically powerful instrument of observation at the Southern Hemisphere. More specifically, Australia. More specifically, Queensland. More specifically, Brisbane. More specifically, the suburb of Herston. Even more specifically, through the window and into bed seven of the Royal Women's and Children's Hospital maternity ward. There they would see Ingrid and her baby boy, Max. This story is not about them. However, if our alien pervert were to shift their instrument of observation slightly to the left there they would see Daphne and her baby boy, Thomas. This story is about him. Thomas Thompson Junior. Obviously named after his father, who had been named after his father, who had been named after his father… [*et cetera*]

> *He walks in a line, devolving through Homo sapiens, Neanderthal man and into an ape. He crouches and scratches himself, eating fleas/lice.*

In fact, by a strange quirk of fate that had become some sort of genetic memory, all the men on that side of the family had all been named Thomas since time immemorial. Or to be more accurate, since the Paleolithic era about 2.6 million years ago with the first of those Thomases who wasn't Thomas so much as [*like an ape*] 'ooh-ah'.

He evolves back along the line, becoming modern man again.

Which made Thomas, the one who had just been born, Thomas the 83,333rd or thereabouts. This story about him begins on a Tuesday. A mild-mannered and unsuspecting Tuesday. The Clark Kent, if you will, of Tuesdays.

He draws a liturgical weekly calendar on the floor. A chime as he becomes TUESDAY.

TUESDAY: Hello. Tuesday. I'm a day of the week. I'm the second day of the working week but the third of the liturgical which starts on Sunday. My name comes from the Old English *Tiwes daeg*, named after the Norse word for their god, Tyr, who was like Mars or Ares, a god of war.

He growls, trying to be ferocious. Fails.

I like: being organised, post-it notes and dry toast. I pick up the slack after Monday a lot.

A chime as he becomes MONDAY, *looking around, hung-over and lost, shielding his eyes from the bright lights.*

MONDAY: Monday.

TUESDAY: I dislike, well, I'm not overly fond of Friday.

A chime and he becomes FRIDAY, *drunk. He grabs his crotch and gives everyone the finger.*

FRIDAY: Fuckin' Friday!

TUESDAY: I'm not overly popular. I am trying to rectify this by offering cheap DVDs, movies and pizza. I don't mind.

NARRATOR: Little did our unsuspecting Tuesday know that it was about to become a lot more interesting than it had ever imagined.

He lies down in bed, becoming THOM.

An annoying digital alarm sounds. THOM *wakes with a start and looks around, realising much to his horror that he's awake. He looks for his alarm clock and when he can't find it, draws a digital display clock with chalk and hits it. The alarm stops.*

At the start of the day, Thom woke up. Which is a good way to start the day. In fact it occurred to Thom that starting your day without waking up could be difficult. Possibly fatal.

THOM *faces the audience, sleepy. A chime.*

THOM: Thomas Thompson Junior. Age 31. I work in I.T. I like: astronomy, the sound that rulers make when you flick them on the edge of a desk and cheese and pickled onion sandwiches before bed. I dislike: most of the dreams I've been having lately, flying and allocated seating at the cinema.

THOM *gets ready for work as the* NARRATOR *narrates.*

NARRATOR: And so it came to pass that our little baby Thomas, the 83,333rd or thereabouts grew up to be an average guy. Chances are you know him. Chances are you are him. Or him if he were a her. For the purposes of this story Thom looks conveniently like your Narrator. Same size, same height. Which is not to say that he is the Narrator. That would be weird. Roaming around in your own home talking about yourself in the third person in past tense to a group of people who aren't really there. Fourth wall comedy. Thom got up, got dressed for work, all the while musing on the latest in a long line of strange dreams probably brought on by cheese and pickled onion sandwiches before bed.

He proceeds to act out the dream as he talks.

This one had involved a group of cats who, having seen the clip for Prince's 'Raspberry Beret' on 'rage', decided to build themselves a man-suit that they could pilot from the inside—like a man-shaped Voltron piloted by cats. The cats drove their man-suit down to the local HMV, bought themselves a copy of 'Around the World in a Day', went home, put it on and danced.

He counts in some music and stops just short of dancing. He gets on a bus instead.

On his way to work, Thom wondered how it was cats had money to buy an album. He hopped off the bus, passed his nemesis The Human Statue…

A chime. The NARRATOR *freezes as* THE HUMAN STATUE. *Then continues.*

… and went to work.

3. HIS BOSS

MEL *points, clicks and winks. The reactions of the other character are implicit.*

MEL: Thom! Thom-boy! Thom-ato! How they hanging, buddy?

A chime.

Melvin Ellis. Mel. The Big M. Mel-u-min-i-um. The Mel-ennium Falcon. I'm a supervisor and trainer at Thom's work. I also do a bit of improv on the side. I like: good bourbon, *Zoo Magazine*, and the fine films of Angelina Jolie. I dislike: fat chicks.

NARRATOR: Mel was a dick. A great big dick. Which is not to say that Mel had a great big dick. In fact if personality was any indicator of size, Mel was hung like a cashew. The only reason Thom put up with his annoying banter and general banality was that it seemed that Mel was happy to do no actual supervising. Which meant that Thom's secret was safe. You see, the truth was Thom had absolutely no idea what he did for a living. He'd done IT at his mother's insistence.

MOTHER: Forget astronomy, Thom. IT. IT's the way of the future. IT's a safe secure job.

NARRATOR: Thom's mum told terrible puns.

He brings out an overhead projector and projects an image of graphs and statistics.

So Thom had studied IT and taken the first job that was offered to him out of university without really bothering to check what they did. He figured he'd work it out in a week or two. Then weeks became months. And the months went to parties, got drunk, shacked up with each other and begat years. By which time it was too late to ask anyone what they did. There was paper and statistics. Thom dutifully gathered this data and turned it into reports and charts without having to understand any of it. This did not come, however, without paranoia.

The NARRATOR *lifts the projector lens into his face, film noir style.*

MEL: So anyway, buddy, can I get an ETA on those AIFs, QAZIs and BZTs? Terry, the CI from CBT, wants them ASAP and on the QT, he's already more than a little POed about the results of that last GSA.

NARRATOR: So Tom mastered being neither good enough to get noticed nor bad enough to warrant attention—a tightrope-walking act of average-ness that took up way more of his time than any of the reports or charts that he was asked to make.

MEL: One more thing, buddy. I can't help but notice that you've been an A04 for like ten years now and that just doesn't seem fair to me. So I had a chat to Terry, the CI from CBT, and he wants to have a chat with you on Friday. Yeah, yeah, yeah. No need to thank me. It'll just be a quick 'coffay' and a chat about what you do, what we do and what you think about what we do. Okay-pokey? Smell you later.

THOM *mouths 'Fuck'.*

NARRATOR: Boy. Tick.

4. GIRL

The NARRATOR *draws the second apartment as he talks.*

NARRATOR: Consider radio waves. Now, like light, radio waves are a form of electromagnetic radiation and so they too travel at our wonderful understood constant of 1,079,252,848.(what?) kilometres per hour. Which means that if our alien pervert happened to have a radio telescope they might now be picking up this:

> *Disco music plays. Cheesy disco light abounds. The* NARRATOR *dances as he attempts to enact the next sequence involving both characters and a crowded dance floor.*

In 1979 this was the favourite song of one Demis Papadopoulous. Demis didn't have time to worry about alien perverts and fantastical technology.

DEMIS: Pfah!

NARRATOR: Because he had spent the whole night dancing with a lovely lady named Kathleen. And against all expectations she had agreed to come home with him. Here's how it happened.

DEMIS: I am Demis.

KATHLEEN: What?

DEMIS: Demis. Papadopoulos. It's Greek. Very common. Like Jones.

KATHLEEN: Kathleen. Jones.

DEMIS: Nice to meet you, Kathleen. I like your pants.

KATHLEEN: What?

DEMIS: Your pants. I like them.

> *The* NARRATOR *stops the scene.*

NARRATOR: Consider for a moment, the sheer unlikely good fortune that must have come about to allow all of Demis Papadopoulos and Kathleen's ancestors to have lived long enough to mate. That at no point did any of them get stabbed, shot, eaten, blown up or eat the wrong berry before they reached sufficient physical maturity to do so. Add to that that Demis somehow managing to survive 'the pants comment' and the odds of Kathleen Jones stumbling in the front door of Demis Papadopoulos' flat with her high heels in her hand would make Pascal's head explode. Nine months later, they had a baby girl. This story is about her.

> *A bell starts to ring insistently, waking* ALETHEA. *She wakes, draws an old analogue clock and slaps it. It continues to ring. She draws the hands onto the clock and hits it again. The alarm bell stops. A chime.*

ALETHEA: Alethea Jones. Alethea's Greek. It means 'truth'. I'm 29 years' old. I'm a writer and illustrator of children's books. I like: sleeping in, riding my bicycle Penelope, playing on my computer Dave and naming inanimate objects. I dislike: the morning, [*air-quotes*] 'self-help', [*air-quotes again*] 'these', and people who call me Althea.

NARRATOR: Alethea, when at all possible, tried to avoid starting the morning altogether. Like fat people avoid salads or coeliacs avoid wheat. In fact maybe that was it, she thought, as she stared at her puffy and deformed morning face in the mirror. Maybe she was just morning intolerant. That would explain the gas. For the purposes of this story, Alethea also looks like your Narrator. Which is not to say that Thom and Alethea look the same. That would be very weird. It's only me who looks the same. As myself.

> *The* NARRATOR *is confused, but decides to continue.*

Alethea's first children's book, entitled *Building Better Monsters*, had won her some reasonable acclaim and a couple of awards. She had always wanted to be a writer and getting to set her own hours of work to avoid the morning altogether was no small part of it. Alethea had long ago realised that there were in fact two types of people in the world. Night-time people, like herself. And morning people, like her publisher, Marko.

A chime. MARKO *does slow annoying and grossly sexual lunges.*

MARKO: Marko Grosetti, 37 years' old. I am a publisher. I like: exploiting artists using my general business arts degree and complete lack of talent and their complete lack of business acumen, tight running shorts and the morning—it's my favourite time of day.

The NARRATOR *takes out pink bike handlebars with basket and streamers attached.*

NARRATOR: Alethea put her beloved notebook (that was about to become incredibly important to this story, so keep up) into the parcel basket of her bicycle Penelope and rode off to an early morning breakfast meeting at her publisher's. Tired, half asleep, and more than a little pissed off at having to endure food she didn't want with a man she didn't like at an hour that she wasn't overly familiar with, Alethea took a wrong turn and ended up going down a myriad of West End back streets before realising seven minutes later that she was in fact lost and late. Which are two things you never want to be because that means you're in the wrong place at the wrong time. And there, high above her head in a tree, in his nest made of human hair and the skin of babies, The Magpie of Montague Road stirred. The Magpie of Montague Road was a black-feathered demon!

He projects a dull scientific drawing of a magpie on the overhead projector.

Yeah. Fucking terrifying! Its blood-red eyes were as cold and dead as the myriad of small dogs it had harried and devoured. It was perpetually randy and had testicles the size of kiwifruit.

He puts a large picture of kiwifruit on the overhead projector, placing them under the magpie. The sizes don't quite match.

Rumour has it that it had once killed an ibis and raped its dead corpse.

He puts up a picture of an ibis and makes the magpie image have sex with it.

It was sitting in its nest in its tree of doom, thinking evil bird-thoughts when the late and lost Alethea Jones rounded the corner onto Montague Road, and with a cry that could loosely be translated as 'Die, stinking ape, die', it leapt from its nest like a fistful of feathers and broken glass and went straight towards Alethea Jones.

He takes the transparent sheet of the magpie drawing and flicks it around in the air, creating the actual bird swooping around ALETHEA's *head.*

Alethea ducked and weaved, desperately trying to remember the advice she had been given on how to avoid attacks from magpies.

A chime.

MAGPIE EXPERT: In the event of being attacked by a magpie, the best I advice I can give you is to hop off your bike and face the magpie down.

ALETHEA: What?!

NARRATOR: Against several millennia of successful survival instincts, Alethea threw down the bicycle and faced off against the magpie. The magpie landed…

He throws the transparency. It eventually lands.

… there. Alethea stood frozen. The magpie pointed its bloodstained beak at her lean olive-skinned throat. Alethea didn't move. The magpie cooed a charming little tune in its throat.

We hear a cute and charming magpie song.

Loosely translated as, 'You don't know it yet but I'm going to kill you and fuck you in the ear'. Alethea didn't dare move. The magpie leapt at her face. Fortunately at that moment a one-eyed Scottish cab driver, clutching a Bible and crucifix, got between Alethea and the bird.

SCOTTISH CABBIE: The power of Christ compels you back to hell!

A chime. The SCOTTISH CABBIE *faces the audience.*

One-eyed William MacCabbie. Taxi driver and lay preacher. I'm 87 years' old. I like: soft toffees, tartan, Ronnie Corbett and Christ.

[*Thumbs up for Christ*] I dislike: hard toffees, plaid, Ronnie Barker [*spits*] and the demon bird who took my eye!

The SCOTTISH CABBIE *forces the magpie back to its tree. The* NARRATOR *puts the magpie transparency back on the overhead projector.*

NARRATOR: One-Eyed William drove the Magpie back into its tree...

SCOTTISH CABBIE: I am strong with the Lord and the power is mine! I am strong with the Lord and the power is mine! Get up there, ya little fucker!

NARRATOR: ... where it sat, glowering and spitting curses in what was probably Aramaic. He helped Alethea into the back of his cab. And as they drove off Alethea looked out of the back window to see her beloved bicycle Penelope receding in the distance. The magpie landed on it.

He puts up an image of the bike, Penelope. Again the size doesn't quite match.

And stared at her, daring her to try and get it back.

5. HER PUBLISHER

NARRATOR: Seven minutes later, Alethea arrived at her breakfast meeting.

MARKO *leans over* ALETHEA'*s chair, doing lunges at her and, not accidentally, sending his crotch repeatedly in the direction of her face.*

MARKO: Althea! Hey there, little lady. Little bit late, are we? Not to worry. Isn't this weather beautiful? I was up at four o'clock this morning. Went for a run and a swim. Did my taxes. And made love to my wife. Now I'm here. [*Seemingly offering his crotch*] Breakfast? It's the most important meal of the day.

NARRATOR: Alethea was 87 percent sure he was picturing her naked.

MARKO *stares at her, picturing her naked.*

MARKO: So, you've got a reading and signing of *Building Better Monsters* at the State Library tomorrow. And this Friday the first draft of the new book is due. And after all of the money that I've put into it, I cannot wait to read it.

ALETHEA *shifts in her chair, uncomfortable.*

NARRATOR: Alethea hadn't finished her new book. Alethea hadn't started her new book. Alethea had gone to start the new book and had been puzzled by a troubling little thought. What if it was no good? What if you're a one-hit wonder? That's easy, she thought. I'll just make it perfect. She hadn't written a word since. She had a title. A promising title. A title that spoke volumes of promise of the whole enterprise. *The Man With Ideas Coming Out of His Ears*. Unfortunately, since putting those clever little words together, she hadn't had a single syllable come out of her left nostril. Her work thus far consisted of two things. An empty file on her computer Dave… [*draws* DAVE *the computer*] entitled 'Difficult Second Album'. And her beloved notebook. Full of sketches, drawings and ideas. Every day for Alethea began with a cup of coffee and a slow turning of its pages, desperately waiting for inspiration to punch her in the face. At that moment, two thoughts raced from the recesses of Alethea's brain, elbowing each other out of the way to reach her consciousness first. The one that arrived first was that today was Tuesday and in one, two, three, four days on Friday she would have broken her contract with a major publisher, bringing her promising young career to a fatal end. The second was that her beloved notebook was still in the parcel basket of her bicycle Penelope, which was last seen in the clutches of the demon bird. Alethea excused herself to go the bathroom and ran like hell from the building.

ALETHEA *looks at the projection of the magpie, high in its tree.*

She kept her distance and stared up into the tree. The magpie was hopping around in a strange tangle of branches. And then she saw. They weren't branches. It was her bicycle Penelope, hoisted up on high. Now, it is perfectly conceivable that someone in a fit of panic had grabbed the bicycle and thrown it at the magpie in a desperate attempt to escape. However, to Alethea's terrified imagination, it was all too conceivable that the little big-balled bastard had gotten it up there himself. The notebook was safe for now, hidden in the parcel basket against the trunk of the tree. But for how long? Without her notebook, she was lost. But without her life, she'd be dead. Alethea trudged home, her cheeks stinging as she tried to hold back tears. Her only consolation was that she had in fact been right all along. Mornings are fucked. [*Beat.*] Girl. Tick.

6. WALL

The NARRATOR *draws a wall between the two apartments.*

NARRATOR: So, that's them. Thom and Alethea. And this is the wall that separates their apartments in a quiet little apartment block in a quiet-er end of West End. They'd never met, never spoken. The briefest of 'hellos'. They came home from their surprisingly crap Tuesdays, the weight of their oncoming Fridays hanging over their heads. They flicked on their lights and kicked off their shoes. Thom walked straight towards the adjoining wall. You see Thom loved astronomy. He had always wanted to be an astronomer. He could think of nothing better than gazing up into the heavens and staring into the past. Thom was hunting supernovae. The death of a star. An explosion equal to one hundred billion suns. Supernovae are incredibly rare, occurring in each galaxy only every one to two hundred years and then only visible to the naked eye if you happened to be in the right part of the galaxy at the right time. Not too far away or you won't see it and not too close or the radiation will kill us all. And only visible for a month or so at the most, the faintest glimmer that shouldn't be there. Finding one is like walking onto a beach and finding a grain of sand that that doesn't belong. In spite of this, Thom lived in hope. He memorised star charts and covered his walls in glow-in-the-dark stars, turning his room into a fully immersive map of the visible universe.

> *He puts a star chart on the overhead projector, creating a field of stars on Thom's walls.*

Once a week, every week, Thom would go to the Herculean and intricate effort of moving each and every one of those stars as it had moved in the sky above.

> *He holds a star in his hand, stroking it.*

And so it was, on that surprisingly crap Tuesday, the weight of his oncoming Friday and his meeting with Terry, the CI from CBT, hanging over him, that Thom stood at the wall, moving the universe, millions of miles between him and Alethea.

> *He goes to* DAVE.

Alethea came home, turned on her computer Dave, entered her

password and sat staring at the blank screen for seven minutes before feeling sick to her stomach. She got her paints and walked to the adjoining wall.

He removes the star field and projects a blank light onto Alethea's walls.

Alethea was painting a mural on the wall. She did it when she was tired or stressed. Or to be more honest, when she was trying to avoid her computer Dave, and her complete lack of new ideas. It was to be a perfect mirror image of her apartment. It wouldn't have the slightest mistake. Not a single thing was left out of place that might ruin the mirror effect. Like Thom and his home-brew planetarium, it made her happy. So that's who they are and where they are, when a remarkably strange thing occurred.

He moves to the WALL *between the apartments.*

The wall between their apartments was a young wall. And like all young walls, it was a romantic and had decided that these two belonged together. Unfortunately, being an inanimate object meant that matchmaking was difficult. So it was going to do the only thing it could think of. It was going to fall down.

The WALL *strains. He stops and catches his breath, then strains again.*

CEILING: [*highly strung*] Hey. Hey, hey. What are you doing?
WALL: Who's that?
CEILING: It's me. The ceiling.
WALL: Oh. Hi, Ceiling.
CEILING: What are you doing?
WALL: Nothing.
CEILING: It doesn't feel like nothing.
WALL: I'm going to fall down.
CEILING: What?!
WALL: No, no, no. It's for love.
CEILING: I don't care what it's for! Think about me. I'll fall.
NARRATOR: At that moment, the floor chimed in.
FLOOR: [*kind of dopey*] Hey, guys. What are you doing?
WALL: Nothing.
FLOOR: Oh. That's right. I'm the floor. Walk all over me.

WALL: If you must know, I just think these two would be a lot happier if there wasn't a wall between them.

CEILING: That's all very well and good but have you thought about me? My structural integrity? I'll fall.

FLOOR: Hey, Wall. What's that?

WALL: What's what?

FLOOR: That.

NARRATOR: And they all looked at Wall. And Wall looked at himself.

The WALL *crosses his eyes.*

And there, spreading across him, ten centimetres long and growing, was a crack.

CEILING: Oh, great! We're all going to die! I hope you're happy!

WALL: No, no, no. I can stop it. There. It's stopped. But. I don't think it's going to stay stopped unless you, Ceiling, and you, Floor, and the rest of the apartments promise to help get these two together.

NARRATOR: Thom stared at the wall. The Groombridge 34 binary system of glow-in-the-dark stars trembled in his hand. There was a crack in the universe. And there was light coming from it.

Light shines from the NARRATOR*'s hand, into* THOM*'s face.*

Alethea stared at the crack in her perfect mural. She tried to paint over it. She tried to fix it. She made it worse. She moved away, afraid of ruining it any further. Thom stared at the inter-dimensional crack that was now spilling light and colour into his room for another seven and a half minutes before needing immediate salty, sour comfort, he made himself a cheese and pickled onion sandwich and went to bed.

7. AN INTERLUDE

NARRATOR: Let us now move back through space and time to a distant star called RS Ophiuchi. Two stars actually. A binary system containing a white dwarf and red giant, dancing together incredibly close but not yet touching. When they do, RS Ophiuchi will become spectacular evidence of the laws of thermodynamics in action. Entropy on an operatic scale. One of Thom's supernovae. The light from that explosion is going to travel for the next four to five thousand light years. So we can either wait for it or get on with the show. All in favour of waiting for it?

He waits.

All in favour of getting on with the show?

He waits.

Let's get on with the show.

> *He takes off a shoe and pulls off a sock, creating a sock puppet of* THOM, *who wakes from a dream.*

In the middle of the night Thom woke in a dream to discover that he was a sock puppet.

SOCK THOM: Gah!

NARRATOR: Not only was Thom a sock puppet, but it seemed that no-one else was.

SOCK THOM: Hey.

NARRATOR: Suddenly, it was Friday and it was time for his meeting with Terry, the CI from CBT.

> TERRY *appears in giant shadow form.*

SHADOW TERRY: So! Thom Thompson Junior! What do you contribute to our company?

SOCK THOM: I have no idea.

> SHADOW TERRY *laughs.*

Oh, God. I'm fired, aren't I?

SHADOW TERRY: Fired? That's the most honest response I've ever had. I'm promoting you to Owner and CEO! What we do now is in your hands.

> SHADOW TERRY *laughs and fades as* SOCK THOM *screams in horror.*

NARRATOR: And so, Sock Thom was being sent to Sydney to run the company. So his friends were throwing him a going-away party, the theme of which was great things from Christian Slater films. Sock Thom roamed his home dressed as the Poisoned Bible from *The Name Of The Rose* by Umberto Eco amidst the strains of 'Wave of Mutilation (UK Surf)' by the Pixies from *Pump Up The Volume*. He thanked all of his friends for coming, some of whom he had never met.

SOCK THOM: Welcome. Thanks for coming.

Another sock puppet appears, this time one of ALETHEA. SOCK THOM *stares at her.*

You're a sock.

SOCK ALETHEA: Yep.

SOCK THOM: I'm a sock.

SOCK ALETHEA: Uh-huh.

SOCK THOM: We're both socks!

She ignores him. He walks away, dejected. She watches him, feels bad and stops him from going.

SOCK ALETHEA: Hey, wait. Cool party. Who are you dressed as?

SOCK THOM: Me? I'm the Poisoned Bible from *Name of the Rose*. But I keep having to explain it to people. You?

SOCK ALETHEA: Winona. From *Heathers*. Like every other girl here.

NARRATOR: And they laughed. And talked. And danced. All through the night. And then, as the morning came, they sat out the back by the Hills hoist and watched as the sun came up. Not saying anything. Just being there. And Thom didn't want to leave anymore. But it was time for him to go. They kissed their goodbyes.

The puppets kiss. Then pash.

And the Sock Girl was carried away by a small black-and-white bird but didn't seem to mind. So Sock Thom was sent to Sydney to run the company. But he couldn't get the girl from the party out of his head. So he filled the hole in his heart with cigarettes, booze and cheap, cheap, Sydney women.

He goes down on SOCK THOM.

He had all the success his mother had ever wanted for him. And all the success he'd ever wanted for himself. But he couldn't get the girl from the party out of his head.

SOCK THOM: Winona!

SOCK THOM *collapses in drunken tears.*

8. THE EXPANSION OF THE UNIVERSE

The NARRATOR *moves across to a* POWER BOX, *already drawn in chalk in the corner.*

NARRATOR: That same night, the building's power box was having issues of its own. Here's what was troubling it.

The NARRATOR *draws a question mark over* POWER BOX *and sits under it.*

POWER BOX: Consider the expansion of the universe. Now, this expansion is held to have started at what we know colloquially as the big bang. An expansion or inflation of unimaginable size and power. Of fire and dust and fire, spilling out. Planets and stars spin into form and shape. And that expansion should just keep going. However, according to some theorists, that expansion will slow, stop, and then reverse. Everything coming back together. Planets, stars, light waves, radio waves, everything back coming together in one final booming collapse. And what happens then, wondered Power Box, all night every night, in his dingy little corner out by the bins. When all the pieces finally come together, what happens then?

9. WEDNESDAY

A chime.

WEDNESDAY: Wednesday! I'm a day of the week! I like motivating people! And posters of kittens hanging from trees. Hang in there, tiger. I dislike the term 'Hump Day'. That's a bit yucky. And I'm not overly fond of Friday.

FRIDAY, *now more drunk, grabs his crotch and gives everyone the finger.*

FRIDAY: Fukkinn' Friddaay!

WEDNESDAY *pumps a fist in the air with a smile to the audience.*

WEDNESDAY: Excelsior!

NARRATOR: That morning Wall, Ceiling, Floor and the rest of the apartments had come up with a plan to get Alethea and Thom together. It involved the doors (not the band, the actual doors). For them, getting people together was pretty much open and shut. It was simply a matter of timing. And so Thom got up, got dressed for work, all the while musing on his long line of strange dreams probably brought on by cheese and pickled onion sandwiches before bed. He stared at the inter-dimensional crack in his wall, shook his head and went to leave his apartment.

THOM *tries to open the door. It is stuck.*

DOOR 1: Okay, I've got him. Door Number Two, where's she?

DOOR 2: I'm not really sure about 'Door Number Two' business. It connotes poorly. Number Two means poo.

DOOR 1: Fine. 'Other Door'.

DOOR 2: Other? Hmmm.

DOOR 1: 'Door'. Where is she?

DOOR 2: She's still in bed.

NARRATOR: Alethea was still in bed. She hadn't slept a wink. The guy next door had been screaming 'Winona' in his sleep all night. Thom took a run-up.

THOM *shoulder charges* DOOR 1.

DOOR 1: Ow! Tell me that woke her up.

DOOR 2: Nup!

NARRATOR: Thom grabbed a chair.

THOM *grabs a chair, holds it above his head, and runs at* DOOR 1.

DOOR 1: That does it. I'm letting him out!

DOOR 1 *opens.* THOM *runs through the doorway and stops, holding the chair above his head and looking around.*

THOM: Morning.

THOM *backs into his apartment, confused. To cover his confusion he pretends that the chair above his head was all part of a fitness plan. He catches the bus.*

NARRATOR: On his way to work, Thom passed his nemesis, The Human Statue.

The NARRATOR *freezes as* THE HUMAN STATUE. *Then continues.*

MEL: Thom! Thom-boy! Thom-ato! How they hanging, buddy? So have you read the weekly report yet? Like I said, buddy, you've got to get in here early and read the weekly report before you start work.

NARRATOR: It occurred to Thom that reading the weekly report was in and of itself, work. Which begged the question: 'How do I work before work?' If I work before work I'm already in fact working and can never reach a state before work in which it was being suggested that I should work. Instead of saying any of this, Thom lied.

THOM: Yes. I read it.

MEL: Yeah, that's right. Rec day.

THOM: What?

MEL: Rec day! You my friend, are taking a rec day on Friday. So am I and I think you'll find the rest of the team is joining us. Friday? Ah, shit. Your meeting with Terry, the CI from CBT. Ah, look mate. I reckon we're just going to have to cancel that meeting.

> *Ridiculously happy music plays.* THOM *dances like a madman. The music stops.*

NARRATOR: Thom was suspicious. Things this good didn't happen to him.

THOM: Why, Mel?

MEL: You my friend, are going to get some culture into you. My improv troupe are putting together a 24-hour theatre-sport extravaganza to take our show *Mission Improv-ible* to Edinburgh. Tickets are forty bucks a pop. And you, my friend, have got to come. How many should I put you down for?

> THOM *stares at* MEL *as sad (cheesy) emotional music plays for a long, long time.*

NARRATOR: Thom weighed up his options. Twenty-four hours of amateur theatre sports or the meeting that would end his career.

THOM: Sorry, Mel. I really think I should have that meeting.

MEL: Okay-pokey. Smell you later.

> MEL *walks away, insulted.*

> ALETHEA *wakes, sleepy.*

NARRATOR: After her usual battle with consciousness had ended in stalemate, Alethea, depressed at the thought of spending another day staring at her computer Dave, stared at her computer Dave and got depressed. She then realised with fifteen minutes to spare that she was due at the State Library for the reading and signing of *Building Better Monsters* that Marko the annoying publisher had set up. She ran into the bathroom, turned on the shower, brushed her teeth, jumped into the shower, slipped, hit her head, rolled, landing in a pile of clothes, making her smell worse than she had before. She put some of it on, raced out of the door, tried to catch the bus, missed the bus and kept running. And ended up arriving fifteen minutes later at the State Library but having not eaten for the last 36 hours, passed out on the spot.

ALETHEA *collapses to the floor. The exhausted* NARRATOR *lies there, catching his breath.*

Oh, yeah. That feels good. [*Beat.*] When she came to, she was surrounded by children and concerned parents. Alan, the lovely, though somewhat Gothic, librarian assistant, helped her into a chair, got a cup of coffee and proceeded to dunk five Iced Vovos into it and jammed them into her mouth. Alethea was deemed too ill to perform, so the reading of *Building Better Monsters* was left up to Alan, the lovely, though somewhat Gothic, librarian assistant.

A chime. ALAN *steps forward.*

ALAN: Alan Rack. I am 37 years' old. I'm a Librarian Assistant, mediaeval recreationist and writer of supernatural erotic fiction. I like: renaissance fencing, my band 'Velvet Angst' and my cat Battle Cat. I dislike: sunlight, the work of Stephenie Meyer (she is fucked!) and deodorant.

He clears his throat, looks around nervously and begins to read Building Better Monsters.

Building Better Monsters by Althea Jones.
>   'There's something under Ivy's bed,
>   She knows it's there for sure.
>   Last night she heard a scratching sound,
>   Like talons on the floor.

>   'Tonight her toy bear growls with fright,
>   Its one eye scans the room.
>   Her mother says, 'It's nothing, dear',
>   Leaving Ivy to her doom.

ALAN*'s voice gets scarier, more horror-film-esque.*

>   'Summoning her courage,
>   Ivy dives beneath the bed.
>   And there she sees the Mirror World.
>   And in it, She. Is. DEAD!'

ALAN *leans over the children, terrifying them.* ALETHEA *watches, horrified.*

NARRATOR: Alethea had always held that her book was a safe scare. Like the so-called scary TV shows of her childhood. 'Doctor Who'. 'Trapdoor'. 'Count Duckula'. The heroine starts off terrified but conquers her fears with the power of imagination. All of this was lost on the crowd of parents, who dragged their crying and screaming children from the building and spent the rest of the day on the phone to her publisher Marko.

MARKO *is on the phone.*

MARKO: Althea. Hey there, little lady. Look, we've run into a spot of trouble. *Building Better Monsters*? Parent groups want it banned from the shelves. Yeah. Not out of moves yet, though. I told them you had a new book due on Friday and they could have a read of the first draft. Contextualise things for them. So do me a favour, sweet-cheeks. Don't fuck it up. Knock it out of the park. Call me!

10. THE SINGING UNIVERSE

NARRATOR: That night Alethea stood in her kitchen stirring her broccoli and onion soup, thinking she should have paid more attention at the greengrocer's. She stirred and hummed the tune she hummed when she stirred.

ALETHEA *hums.*

Thom trudged home. He flicked off the lights. He kicked off his shoes. He stared at the inter-dimensional crack in his wall. And heard the most beautiful music coming from it. He sat down and listened, dreaming of a better place. Somewhere on the other side of the universe.

THOM *sits and listens. The music hangs in the air, full of potential.*

Alethea drank her broccoli and onion soup, which tasted disappointingly like broccoli and onion.

The NARRATOR *peels* DAVE *off the back wall. He's just cardboard, complete with a chalk-drawn Apple Mac symbol on the back.*

She got her computer Dave, and sat with her back against the wall and stared at him. Now, it should be noted that all this was giving

Dave a bit of a complex. Every day, a beautiful woman stared at him like he was the most useless piece of crap on earth. All of his paranoid fantasies were rapidly evolving into one major neurosis. Alethea stared at Dave.

DAVE: Argh!

NARRATOR: And hummed. Thom listened. The Wall got excited.

WALL: This was it. Contact.

NARRATOR: They both fell asleep.

WALL: Poop!

11. THE LAST STAND—PART I

A chime and the NARRATOR *becomes* THURSDAY.

THURSDAY: Thursday. I'm old. I'm tired. I just want it over. I like Saturday. Why can't I be Saturday? I could be Saturday. Have a coffee, read a paper, push a mower. Fuck. I dislike... him.

> FRIDAY, *now extremely drunk, grabs his crotch and gives the finger.*

FRIDAY: Fukkkinnn... Frii...

> FRIDAY *vomits on* THURSDAY*'s foot.*

THURSDAY: Do you have any idea what it's like spending your entire existence next to that? You don't, do you? No. [*Beat.*] Fuck off.

NARRATOR: Thom woke from a surprisingly restful and dream-free sleep. This was it. Today was Thursday. Tomorrow Friday and his meeting with Terry, the CI from CBT, that would end his career. Today was his last chance to find out what the hell it was he did for a living. On the way to work Thom punched his nemesis in the nuts.

> THOM *punches* THE HUMAN STATUE *in the nuts.* THE HUMAN STATUE *remains unmoved. Then, quietly moans.*

When he got to work, something was odd. Mel was exercising.

> MEL *exercises on a (not-so-much visible) walking machine.*

THOM: Hi, Mel. What are you doing?

MEL: [*still annoyed*] Oh. Hi, Thom. Getting my heart rate up. Tomorrow's the big day. Not that you care.

THOM: Oh, no. I care. I'll try and come after work. Can I ask you something?

MEL: Hang on.

> MEL *tries to stop the machine, making it go faster. He walks furiously.*

Ooh, shit.

> *He stops the machine and climbs off.*

Sorry. Uncontrollable mime accident. So what can I do you for? No. Wait. Let's play Alphabetical. Yeah. Get my improv on! Okey-pokey, Thom-boy.

> *A dramatic kung fu gong.* MEL *poses in a lame martial arts stance.*

Ask what you came to ask.

THOM: Okay.

MEL: No, no. Alphabetical. A. B. C. D.

> THOM *thinks.*

THOM: But… it's a difficult question?

MEL: Can't you get on with it?

THOM: Don't rush me.

MEL: Easy for you to say.

THOM: For the last ten years…

MEL: Go on.

THOM: Have you ever…

MEL: I'm listening.

THOM: … just wanted to ask something but you were afraid people might…

MEL: Keep going.

THOM: … laugh at you.

MEL: [*overly sympathetic*] Maaate.

THOM: No.

MEL: Oh.

THOM: Perhaps this just wasn't a good idea.

MEL: Quiet!

> MEL *looks around, pretending he heard something. He points out his clever contribution.*

THOM: Really?

MEL: Sorry.

THOM: The truth is, Mel… I don't know what we do at this company.

MEL: [u] You…

THOM: Very little.

MEL: What?

THOM: Xerox machines. Paper. Statistics. I have been here for ten years and I have no idea what any of it is for and before I have my meeting with Terry, the CI from CBT, I would really appreciate it if someone explained it to me.

MEL: You have no idea what we do here.

THOM: Zero.

NARRATOR: Mel didn't say anything. He just walked away. But the laughter started in the management office, trickled down through the staffroom, into the cubicles, and by the end of the day Thom couldn't go anywhere without hearing the laughter of his workmates echo behind his back. It did not escape his notice that the only place laughter was not coming from was Terry's office. Thom went home.

12. THE LAST STAND—PART II

ALETHEA *wakes with her computer* DAVE, *in her lap.*

NARRATOR: Alethea awoke on this, the last day of her promising young career, with an Enter Key indent in her forehead, and a blank 10,000-page Word document on her computer Dave…

DAVE: … who was having a bit of a nervous breakdown!

NARRATOR: She plugged him into the wall…

DAVE: … much to his relief!

NARRATOR: And having sort of eaten and sort of slept, she knew what she had to do. She was going to kill the Magpie of Montague Road.

He puts on a helmet with dozens of plastic bird attack stems sticking out of it. He turns the overheard projector on, revealing the magpie sitting high in the tree. Dramatic battle music plays.

Alethea marched to directly under the Tree of Doom. The magpie hopped about trying to disembowel the bike. The notebook was still safe, still trapped in the parcel basket of the bicycle against the tree. At that moment the magpie spotted Alethea and with a cry like one of the Nazguls from *Lord of the Rings Trilogy* by JRR Tolkien, it leapt from its nest straight towards Alethea Jones!

He steps out of the action.

Now it should be noted that Alethea has manipulated time and space once before. Her parents, believing in the nutritional value of fruit and vegetables, managed to raise Alethea without letting a single article of refined sugar or food colouring pass her lips. Later, at university and away from home, Alethea went to a party where someone was passing around a large bowl of Skittles. It's university. You try things. Alethea took a handful, put them in her mouth, chewed sensibly 22 times and swallowed. The resulting chemical reaction caused Alethea to vibrate three seconds into the future.

He vibrates three seconds into the future. He notices, then steps back into the action.

At this moment a similar though inverse effect occurred. Adrenaline allowed Alethea to slow time down long enough to produce a can of deodorant and a lighter. She flicked the lighter and pushed the can of deodorant. A plume of flame shot forth…

He takes out an orange transparency to make fire. It looks shit.

That is shit.

He puts the orange transparency on the projector and takes out a long red satin cloth from his pocket, much more excited.

Plume of flame (fuck yeah!) shot forth, immolating the bird. The bird flew high and wide. But Alethea followed. The feathered ball of flame flew. Its flight cut out. It fell, bounced off a roof and landed on the ground. Its burnt, blackened body—dead. Alethea had killed the Magpie of Montague Road.

He looks at the tree projection, now bathed in orange light from the shit transparency.

Alethea turned to see that the whole tree was on fire. She went and stood underneath. The ashes from her beloved notebook fell on her tear-stained face. Eventually, the branches couldn't take it anymore.

And her bicycle Penelope, came crashing to the ground, its bent, broken, buckled body buggered.

He drops the handlebars to the ground.

13. THE LAST STAND—PART III

NARRATOR: The Wall was getting desperate. It got down on its knees (sort of) and prayed. 'Okay, Wall God. It's like this. Although I have an entire universe on one side and a very nice mural on the other, I am but a lowly wall. And I can think of nothing better than getting these two together. And I know I haven't been altogether consistent with my Wall Godly devotions, but if it is within your Wall power to make all the pieces come together as it were, I'd really be grateful and I promise to be a better wall. Thanks. I mean Amen. Armen? Amen. Armen. I don't know. Thanks.'

14. SUBURBAN POWER SURGE BLUES

The NARRATOR *lies in Thom's apartment.*

NARRATOR: Thom lay in his room and stared up into the universe. The Doors had it right (the band, not the actual doors). This was indeed the end. Everyone knew his secret. And the only way to keep his job was to suck up to his boss by enduring 24 hours of amateur theatre sports.
THOM: Oh, God.
NARRATOR: He got dressed, practised smiling in the mirror and went to meet his fate. Four steps outside into the corridor, a group of cats brushed past his leg and he realised that, in his pit of despair, he had forgotten to put on any socks. Sockless Thom walked back indoors.

THOM *turns and heads back inside.*

At that moment Alethea was staring at Dave for what would be the final time. She looked into his shiny and reflective screen, saw her own face staring back at her, reached her lowest point and said…
ALETHEA: I hate you.
NARRATOR: Dave took it personally. He didn't know she was talking to herself. He thought she was talking to him. Unable to live one moment longer with a beautiful woman thinking he was shit, Dave did the only thing he could think of. He overclocked himself by three hundred

percent, loaded every program he had on offer. And thirty seconds later with a gay wheel-of-death system warning…

DAVE: I have always loved you.

NARRATOR: … Dave cooked his motherboard.

DAVE *short-circuits. The lights flicker.*

And that would have been it, had he not been plugged in that morning. The resulting short circuit fed back through the building, down through the wires and into the Power Box, who was still contemplating meaning in a collapsing universe.

He turns the question mark over the POWER BOX *into a light bulb.*

That short circuit set off a metaphorical light bulb over Power Box's head and in that moment he realised…

POWER BOX: … that if all the matter in the known universe was compressed into a single area, the only result could be an explosion, an expansion, another big bang. Life, all over again: expanding, and then eventually contracting and then expanding again. The thought surged on and in that moment Power Box realised that if you sped up the expansion and contraction of the universe sufficiently you would eventually end up with something that resembled… the beating of a human heart. Touched by the heartbeat of the cosmos and the romance of the moment, Power Box did the only thing it could think of to help Wall out. It dropped its safety switches and fed all that power back into the main unit.

The NARRATOR *flicks the switches on* POWER BOX. *The lights snap out, plunging the place into darkness. The lights start fading up slowly throughout the following.*

NARRATOR: Thom froze in the blackened corridor. Alethea searched for candles that she didn't own. Thom put his hand onto the handle of what he thought was his door. Alethea went to check the fuse box.

A projection appears of ALETHEA *and* THOM *kissing. It's quite cute.*

The first thing that touched were their lips. Which is quite hard to do. You should try it. But not now. The resulting kiss set off chemicals in their brains. The kind chocolate gives you. The kind sex gives you. The kind a good idea gives you. Alethea's feelings of creativity transformed into actual ideas. Not just one—hundreds, millions. Ideas, it could be said, fell from her ears. She closed her eyes and pulled Thom closer. Thom kept his eyes wide open. And there, out of Alethea's window, in an area of the sky he would never have seen from his own apartment, he saw RS Ophiuchi going supernova, heralding its death five thousand years ago just for him. And in that moment, Thom realised that his mistake wasn't not liking theatre sports. And it wasn't not knowing what he did for a living. It was settling for a job he didn't want all those years ago. He smiled and pulled Alethea even closer.

15. FIN

The NARRATOR *steps out of the embrace and looks at it, smiling.*

NARRATOR: That's pretty much it. Thom didn't go back to work. He did go to the theatre sports extravaganza long enough to hold up a sign.

> *He lights up a sign on the projector that reads 'I Quit, You Cashew Dick Shithead'.*

Alethea handed in a handwritten copy of her new book with five minutes to spare. I forget what it's about. Thom and Alethea moved in to Alethea's apartment, which is quite sensible considering rental prices in West End. The Wall became a devout believer in the Wall Gods.

> *He looks up at the light bulb still hanging above the space.*

And at night, the light bulbs of the building hum and flicker with a certain serene happiness. Electrical systems are nothing if not romantic.

> *The light bulb fades to darkness as the* NARRATOR *stares at it, smiling peacefully.*

THE END

www.currency.com.au

Visit Currency Press' website now to:

- Buy your books online
- Browse through our full list of titles, from plays to screenplays, books on theatre, film and music, and more
- Choose a play for your school or amateur performance group by cast size and gender
- Obtain information about performance rights
- Find out about theatre productions and other performing arts news across Australia
- For students, read our study guides
- For teachers, access syllabus and other relevant information
- Sign up for our email newsletter

The performing arts publisher

9780868199559